Broccoli by Brody

BROCCOLI
by Brody

Recipes for America's
Healthiest Vegetable

Lora Brody

William Morrow and Company, Inc.

NEW YORK

It is the policy of William Morrow and Company, Inc., and its imprints and affiliates, recognizing the importance of preserving what has been written, to print the books we publish on acid-free paper, and we exert our best efforts to that end.

Library of Congress
Cataloging-in-Publication Data

Brody, Lora, 1945-
        Broccoli by Brody / Lora Brody.
            p. cm.
        Includes index.
        ISBN 0-688-12183-7
        1. Cookery (Broccoli) I. Title.
TX803.B66B76 1993   92-23442
641.6'535—dc20   CIP

Printed in the United States of America

First Edition

1   2   3   4   5   6   7   8   9   1 0

BOOK DESIGN BY RICHARD ORIOLO

To Harriet
and to Lynne, with gratitude

Contents

Introduction

I was a normal kid in the fifties; I hated vegetables. Canned corn and mashed potatoes were about my limit. Anything green was left neglected and wilting on the side of my plate. Threats of all the starving children in China weren't enough to make me try even a nibble. Approaching adulthood did little to convince me that green vegetables were worth eating. Then I went to dinner at my in laws to be. They didn't know they were my in laws to be. I'm not even sure their son knew. But I knew, and that's what counted. I had to make a great impression, right? I dressed right, smiled when I was supposed to, and made bright, articulate conversation. We sat down to dinner. I remembered to put my napkin on my lap; I didn't spill my soup all over the front of my dress; I didn't cut my meat like a three-year-old. Trouble came in the form of a big serving dish full of broccoli that was being passed right toward me. I gulped hard. Was this guy worth going to the unimaginable extreme of actually eating a green vegetable? I took a very small helping. His mother grabbed the serving spoon and heaped on some more, exclaiming that it was her most

sought-after recipe. I was trapped. I cut off a tiny piece, I raised the
fork to my mouth, and said a silent prayer.

Well, you don't have to be a rocket scientist to figure out that
the rest is history. I was an instant convert, and now here I am
actually writing a book that has nothing but broccoli recipes. You
go figure it out. All I know is that this versatile vegetable is delicious
both by itself, simply served steamed with a few drops of lemon
juice, or in elaborate preparations from crepes to casseroles.

Ah, broccoli, how do I love you? Let me count the ways:
roasted with garlic and red peppers, in a pungent pesto sauce,
champagne tempura, tossed with scallops and served with zesty
lemon sauce. . . .

Let the uninitiated eat their peas and beans, leave the masses
to their spuds; those of us in the know are going green—and loving
every bite.

Broccoli by Brody

BROCCOLI
Basics

Fresh broccoli is always available. Take care when selecting a fresh bunch. Just because the color is bright green does not mean it's fresh. If the stems are thick and woody, or the buds are open and look dry and separated, then it's old. If the bunch wilts in your hand when you pick it up, put it down and choose another. Look for tiny, tender buds that are tightly packed, and look for stems that are moist, sturdy, and not dried out, dusty looking, or limp. Since you can utilize all parts of this vegetable, make sure the stems look as good as the buds.

Broccoli rape (rabe or raab) has longer, thinner stems, smaller leaves, and tiny, open yellow buds. All of it is edible, but it has a stronger, more bitter taste than regular broccoli. You can use either one in the recipes in this book.

Chinese broccoli has tiny stems, very small florets, and a healthy abundance of green leaves growing off the stems. This is the only broccoli where the leaves as well as the stems and florets are consumed. The leaves, which make up the bulk of the vegetable, have a mild, pleasing taste. There are several recipes in this collection in which you may substitute Chinese broccoli, which is readily available in Chinese markets and some specialty food shops.

Stored in an airtight plastic bag in the refrigerator, broccoli will keep for one week. If you have broccoli that's past its prime, use it to make soup. While frozen broccoli might be a little more convenient because it's already chopped or cut up, it doesn't have the flavor that fresh broccoli has. It's certainly acceptable for use in these recipes. What I strongly recommend against using is the broccoli that has been precut and is available either in salad bars or placed in individual plastic containers in the supermarket. The former is sprayed with a preservative to keep it fresh and sparkling, and the latter is usually dried out and lacking freshness. You're paying top dollar for inferior produce.

When a recipe calls for a whole stalk of broccoli, slice off the bottom inch of each stalk (more if the stalk looks particularly woody). Remove any leaves attached to the stalks, and then slice lengthwise any stems thicker than 1 inch into two or three pieces, leaving the florets attached or not, according to the recipe directions. Use a sharp paring knife or vegetable peeler to remove the tough outer skin. This step is unnecessary for the thinner stalks. If a recipe calls for Chinese broccoli, leave the leaves attached to the stalks.

When a recipe instructs you to cut the stalks into sections, remember that the more uniform in size the pieces, the better the chances they will be cooked at the same time. If you want large chunks, it is not necessary to cut thick stems into lengthwise pieces first, although you still want to remove the fibrous skin from the outside of the thicker stalks. If a recipe calls for matchstick pieces, trim off the florets, lay the whole stalk down on a cutting board, and cut it in half. Cut each half into several slices, then cut each slice into long, thin strips.

When a recipe calls for florets only, slice off the bushy top of the broccoli, leaving about 2 inches of stalk still attached. Again, any thin stems do not have to be peeled. Reserve the stems for another use. Break the florets into smaller clumps as directed in the recipe.

How to Cook Broccoli

Boiling   Fill a pot large enough to hold all the broccoli comfortably (too big is better than too small) two thirds full with water. Add ½ teaspoon of salt. Place the lid on the pan and bring the water to a rolling boil. Add the broccoli, cover, and cook for 2 minutes or until just tender. You can test this by sticking the tip of a sharp knife into a thick piece It should go in easily. Drain the broccoli in a colander.

Steaming   Place ½ inch of water in the bottom of a large pot. If you have a steamer basket, place it in the bottom of the pan (it is not necessary to use one). Add a pinch of salt, cover, and bring the water to a vigorous boil. Steam for 2 to 3 minutes or until the broccoli is just tender.

These cooking times will result in crisp (al dente) broccoli. If you like yours softer, then increase the cooking time by 1 to 2 minutes. Keep in mind, however, that the longer you cook broccoli, the more vitamins you destroy.

If you are preparing the broccoli for a salad or to use at a later time in a hot dish, then immediately after removing it from the boiling water, run cold water over it to stop the cooking.

Microwaving   It is very important to cut the broccoli into similarly sized pieces when cooking them in the microwave. In a microwave dish, place the broccoli in one layer. Add ½ inch of water and cover the dish with plastic wrap. Microwave on high for 2 to 3 minutes. To avoid a steam burn, remove the plastic wrap carefully from the dish.

*   *   *

No matter what method you choose, some cooks suggest adding a pinch of baking soda to the cooking water to keep the broccoli a brilliant green. I find that it turns the vegetable to mush if you use more than the tiniest amount.

You can barbecue broccoli (page 8) and you can roast it in the oven (page 67). Any way you choose to cook it, I hope you'll be inspired by these recipes to include this delectable, versatile, economical, and healthful vegetable in many, many meals.

It's Healthy Being Green

Since much of the recent attention directed toward broccoli is for health and diet purposes, I have tried to make healthy choices when creating many of these recipes. In most of the recipes the broccoli is cooked a very short time to retain vitamins and nutrients. There are several recipes using raw broccoli, which retains the maximum amount of fiber, which is often lost during cooking. You may substitute low-fat dairy products (milk, cheeses, yogurt, etc.), as well as low-fat broths, polyunsaturated and vegetable spray oils, and, if you wish, egg substitutes, according to individual package instructions. When served with pasta, rice, or legumes, many of these dishes make nourishing and satisfying vegetarian main courses.

Broccoli in Olive Oil

Serves 6

This simple preparation lets the fresh flavor of the broccoli shine through. Take care not to let the garlic brown or it will become bitter.

- 1/2 cup olive oil
- 5 to 6 cloves garlic, finely chopped
- 4 cups broccoli florets, cut into bite-sized pieces and steamed or microwaved for 2 minutes or until just tender
- 1/2 teaspoon dried oregano
- 1/4 cup fresh basil, coarsely chopped
- 1/3 cup grated Parmesan cheese

Heat the oil in a wok over medium-high heat. Add the garlic and sauté until light golden.

Pour over the broccoli and toss until well coated with the oil. Add the herbs, toss with the cheese, and serve.

Grilled Broccoli

Serves 8

A tangy accompaniment to barbecued chicken, fish, or meat, this dish takes only a few minutes to prepare and cook.

- **1 pound broccoli stems and florets, stems peeled**
- **1/2 cup spicy barbecue sauce**
- **2 tablespoons olive oil**

Trim the bottoms of the broccoli stems. Cut the bunch lengthwise into several 3/4-inch-wide pieces and cut each piece into 3/4-inch-thick widths. Steam for 1 minute.

Place the pieces in a shallow baking dish and pour the barbecue sauce over the broccoli. Toss to coat the broccoli. Place the broccoli spears in a barbecue basket or use tongs to place them on a grill.

Grill 3 to 4 inches from the hot coals until the sauce starts to bubble, about 5 minutes. Serve hot.

Broccoli with Mustard-Lemon Sauce

Serves 6 to 8

Perfect in its simplicity, this is a tasty springtime dish to serve with roast lamb or veal.

- 1/2 stick (4 ounces) butter or margarine
- Juice of 1 lemon
- 2 teaspoons Dijon mustard
- 1/2 teaspoon dried tarragon, or 1 tablespoon chopped fresh tarragon
- 4 cups broccoli stems and florets, stems peeled, sliced in thin spears, and steamed or microwaved for 2 minutes or until just tender

Melt the butter in a small saucepan over low heat. Add the lemon juice, mustard, and tarragon. Mix well.

Pour the sauce over the steamed broccoli and serve.

Broccoli Baby Food
Makes about 3½ cups

Here's a lovely way to introduce your baby to the wonders of green vegetables (full of calcium and vitamins). Homemade baby food is so much better than store-bought because you know exactly what's in it. (Be sure to check with your pediatrician before adding broccoli or any other vegetables to your baby's diet.) You can make several cups and freeze the cooled puree in ice-cube trays. Pop out the frozen cubes, store them in Ziploc bags in the freezer, and heat in the microwave.

- ⅔ cup water
- 3 cups (about ⅔ pound) broccoli stems and florets, stems peeled and cut into 1-inch pieces

Bring the water to a boil in a medium-sized saucepan. Add the broccoli, lower the heat to a simmer, and cook, covered, for 10 minutes or until the broccoli is soft.

Use a slotted spoon to transfer the broccoli to the work bowl of a food processor or blender. Process, adding several tablespoons of the cooking liquid, until the mixture is a smooth puree.

BROCCOLI
Soups and
Appetizers

Broccoli, Leek, and Potato Soup

Makes 6 cups

It's hard to believe something this hearty could be so low in calories and fat. With a green salad and bread, this soup makes a simple, satisfying meal.

- 1 tablespoon olive oil
- 2 large leeks, white part only, carefully washed and then chopped into 1/2-inch pieces
- 1 large onion, coarsely chopped
- 1 large carrot, sliced
- 4 cups broccoli stems and florets, stems peeled (reserve 1/4 cup florets for garnish)
- 4 cups canned chicken broth, or 2 vegetable or chicken bouillon cubes dissolved in 4 cups hot water
- 2 medium boiling potatoes, peeled and cut into 1-inch pieces

Sour cream or plain yogurt

Heat the oil in a large, heavy-bottomed pot. Add the leeks and onions and sauté over medium-high heat until tender. Add the carrots and broccoli and sauté for 3 minutes, stirring constantly.

Add the chicken broth and potatoes and bring the liquid to a boil. Reduce the heat, cover, and simmer for 30 minutes.

Puree the mixture in small batches in a blender or food processor. Return the puree to the pot and reheat on low heat.

Garnish each serving with dollops of sour cream and the reserved florets.

Sudanese Red Lentil–Broccoli Soup

Serves 8

This thick soup has just the right combination of spicy flavors. Steamed broccoli is added just before serving to preserve its texture and taste. This is a hearty dish just right for a midwinter meal. It's also great served over rice or couscous.

- 1/4 cup olive oil
- 2 cloves garlic, finely chopped
- 2 cups red lentils, rinsed
- 2 cups finely chopped onions
- 1/4 cup shoyu (Japanese soy sauce) or regular soy sauce
- 4 cups water
- 1/2 teaspoon ground coriander
- 1/2 teaspoon ground cumin
- 1/2 teaspoon freshly ground black pepper
- 3/4 cup feta cheese, crumbled
- 2 cups broccoli stems and florets, stems peeled, cut into 2-inch pieces, and steamed, or microwaved for 2 minutes or until just tender

Heat the olive oil in a large, heavy-bottomed pot. Add the garlic and cook over medium heat until the garlic is soft and translucent.

Add lentils, onions, shoyu, and water to the pot. Cover and cook over medium heat until the water comes to a simmer. Lower the heat and cook for 30 minutes or until the lentils are soft.

Add the spices and feta, re-cover the pot, and continue to

simmer, stirring occasionally, for another 20 minutes.

Puree the mixture in small batches in either the food processor or blender until smooth. Just before serving, stir in the broccoli.

Broccoli Wonton Soup

Serves 4 (about 5 cups including the wontons)

Here is an excellent, quick-to-prepare addition to any meal that needs a lift. If you can't find enoki mushrooms, feel free to substitute any mushrooms of your choice. You can even use dried mushrooms, reconstituting them in hot water first.

- 3 cups chicken broth, or 3 chicken or vegetable bouillon cubes dissolved in 3 cups hot water
- 1 tablespoon fresh ginger, peeled and thinly sliced
- 1 cup watercress, thick stem ends trimmed off, broken into small pieces and firmly packed
- 2 scallions, white and green parts, chopped
- 20 Broccoli Fried Wontons (page 16), uncooked

    Hot chili oil or sesame oil to taste
- 2 ounces enoki (or other mushrooms of your choice)

Heat the broth in a large pot over medium heat. When the liquid comes to a simmer, add the ginger and cook for 5 minutes.

Add the watercress and scallions and cook until the watercress is wilted, about 5 minutes.

Add the wontons, cover, and simmer for 2 to 3 minutes or until the wontons pop to the surface and the wonton skins are no longer transparent.

Add the chili oil to taste. Ladle the soup into bowls and garnish with the mushrooms.

Broccoli Fried Wontons

Makes about 60

These can be fried, steamed, or cooked right in soup (page 15). Since they are a big job, it makes sense to double or triple the recipe and freeze the extra wontons for another time. (To freeze, place on a cookie sheet in one layer and when frozen, seal in heavy-duty plastic bags.) You can chop the vegetables by hand or do it in the food processor. If you do use the processor, take care not to turn the filling to mush by overprocessing it.

- $\frac{1}{2}$ cup finely chopped onions
- 2 teaspoons fresh ginger, peeled and chopped
- 2 cloves garlic, finely chopped
- $1\frac{1}{2}$ cups finely chopped broccoli stems and florets, stems peeled
- $\frac{1}{2}$ cup firm tofu, chopped
- $\frac{1}{4}$ teaspoon freshly ground black pepper
- One 14-ounce package wonton wrappers (3 inches × 3 inches)
- 1 cup vegetable oil

- 2 tablespoons soy sauce
- $\frac{1}{2}$ teaspoon hot Chinese mustard powder

Combine the onions, ginger, broccoli, tofu, and pepper and mix well.

Place 1 teaspoon of the filling in the center of each wonton wrapper. Moisten the edges with water and gather up the four corners to make a tiny pouch. Squeeze the edges to seal.

Heat the oil in a wok or large skillet and fry the wontons, three or four at a time, gently turning them while spooning hot oil over them until they turn crispy and golden brown. Drain on paper towels.

Make a dipping sauce by mixing the soy sauce and Chinese mustard powder together in a bowl until the powder is dissolved.

Broccoli Endive Spears

Makes 30 to 40

Belgian endive, available all year round, makes a lovely base for this elegant finger hors d'oeuvre. You can use low-fat cream cheese or farmer cheese to turn this into a low-fat appetizer or snack.

  3 cups broccoli florets, cut into ½ inch pieces

  3 large heads Belgian endive, 5 inches long

  2 tablespoons each chopped fresh parsley, basil, and
     oregano

  8 ounces whipped cream cheese

  Dash of hot sauce to taste

Steam, or microwave the broccoli for 2 minutes or until just tender. Rinse immediately with cold water to stop the cooking. Set aside.

Trim the root end of the endive to release the leaves. Separate the leaves, reserving the largest for the spears. Use the tiny leaves for salad or for a tasty snack.

In a bowl or food processor, combine the herbs and cream cheese. Blend until smooth and then add the hot sauce to taste.

Place a heaping tablespoon of the filling at the root end of each endive spear and top with a generous cluster of cooked broccoli. Arrange the spears on a platter to serve.

Lemon-Broccoli-Poppyseed Muffins

Makes 12

The zip of lemon and the crunch of poppyseeds combine to make a deliciously different muffin. They freeze beautifully and can be heated either in the microwave or in a conventional oven. These savory treats are a perfect accompaniment to soups and salads.

1 cup all-purpose flour, sifted before measuring

1 cup whole wheat flour, sifted before measuring

1 tablespoon baking powder

½ teaspoon salt

2 tablespoons poppyseeds

2 extra-large eggs

¼ cup vegetable oil

Juice of 1 lemon plus milk to make 1 cup liquid

Finely grated rind of 1 lemon

2¼ cups chopped broccoli stems and florets

Preheat the oven to 400°F. Grease a 12-cup muffin pan or line it with muffin liners.

In a bowl, combine the flours, baking powder, salt, and poppyseeds. Stir to mix well; set aside.

In another bowl, mix together the eggs, oil, milk/lemon juice, and lemon rind. Combine the dry and wet ingredients, mixing gently with a fork until the dry ingredients are just moistened. With a rubber scraper, fold in the broccoli.

Fill each muffin cup half full. Bake for 20 minutes or until the muffins are golden brown.

Broccoli Champagne Tempura

Serves 6 to 8

This delicate batter employs an unusual ingredient and the resulting taste is divine. Plan to serve the tempura immediately after cooking it.

    1 cup brut (dry) Champagne
    1 cup all-purpose flour
  1/4 teaspoon salt
    3 to 4 cups broccoli stems and florets, cut into
       3-inch × 1-inch spears
    1 cup vegetable oil

In a bowl, mix the Champagne, flour, and salt together. Let the batter sit for 30 minutes at room temperature.

Steam or microwave the broccoli for 1 minute, then run it under cold water. It should be al dente but not raw. Drain and pat dry.

Heat the oil in a small saucepan or wok until very hot (375°F). Drop the broccoli spears into the batter one at a time. Stir with a fork until well coated. Drop the spears into the hot oil and fry them, one or two at a time, until they are light golden and crispy. Remove them with a slotted spoon to paper towels. Continue until all the broccoli is done. Serve immediately.

Broccoli Samosas

Makes 20 small or 10 large

Samosas are a type of fried Indian dumpling with a spicy filling that will warm you with its delicious flavors. Serve these after a bowl of soup and you have a great meal. Plain yogurt and mango chutney are perfect garnishes.

- 1 medium potato, peeled and cut into small cubes
- 2 cups chopped broccoli stems and florets, stems peeled
- 1/2 cup frozen peas
- 2 teaspoons vegetable oil
- 1/2 cup finely chopped onions
- 2 cloves garlic, minced
- 2 teaspoons minced fresh ginger
- 2 teaspoons fresh lemon juice
- 1 teaspoon dried coriander, or 2 tablespoons chopped fresh coriander
- 1/2 teaspoon ground cumin
- 2 cups all-purpose flour
- 3 tablespoons margarine
- 1/2 teaspoon salt
- Water
- 1 cup vegetable oil

Put the potato in a saucepan, cover with water, and boil for 10 minutes. Add the broccoli and boil for 5 more minutes. Add the peas, boil for 1 more minute, and drain.

Heat the 2 teaspoons of oil over medium-high heat and sauté the onions, garlic, and ginger until tender. Add the drained vegetables, lemon juice, and spices and toss gently until well mixed. Set aside to cool.

Add the flour, margarine, and salt to a food processor and process until well mixed. While the machine is still running, slowly add the water until a soft dough forms.

Remove the dough and divide it into 20 balls for small samosas. Flatten the small balls into 3-inch circles. To make larger samosas, divide the dough into 10 balls and flatten the balls into 4-inch circles.

Place 1 tablespoon of the vegetable filling on the small circles or 2 tablespoons on the large circles. Lightly moisten the edges of the pastry with water. Fold over the dough to form a semicircle shape and pinch the dough to seal the edges.

Heat the 1 cup of oil in a wok and fry each samosa, spooning hot oil over each until it puffs up. Drain on paper towels and serve immediately.

Broccoli Cheese Melts

Serves 6

This makes a super-fast vegetarian lunch or light supper, or even brunch. It's a dish that your friends and family will request again and again. Feel free to use low-fat cream cheese or farmer cheese.

      Six 5- to 6-inch pita pockets
        6 tablespoons plain or herbed cream cheese
        1 tablespoon olive oil
       10 ounces mushrooms, thinly sliced
        1 cup thinly sliced Spanish onions
        1 clove garlic, minced
        2 cups broccoli stems and florets, stems peeled, cut
           into 1-inch pieces, and steamed or microwaved for
           2 minutes or until just tender
        1 tomato, chopped
        1 cup grated Cheddar cheese
        1 cup tightly packed alfalfa sprouts

Spread each pita pocket with about 1 tablespoon of cream cheese. Set aside. Preheat the broiler.

Heat the oil over medium-high heat in a large, heavy skillet. Add the mushrooms, onions, and garlic and sauté until caramelized to a rich dark brown but not burned and the liquid is evaporated, about 15 to 20 minutes.

Distribute the onion mixture over the pitas. Sprinkle with the broccoli and then the tomato.

Distribute the grated cheese over all and broil 4 inches from the heat for 3 minutes or until the cheese is melted and just starting to brown. Remove the pitas from the broiler and garnish with the sprouts.

Broccoli Pesto

Makes 1 cup

Finally, an economical alternative to traditional pesto—and one that you can make all year round. This lively sauce can be used as a topping on pizza, pasta, fish, chicken, and vegetarian dishes. Try it spread on toasted slices of Italian bread as well. It will keep in a tightly sealed jar for up to two weeks in the refrigerator.

- 1 cup chopped broccoli florets
- 2 cloves garlic, peeled
- 1/4 cup olive oil
- 2 tablespoons fresh lemon juice
- 1/2 cup walnut pieces, pine nuts, or almonds
- 1/4 cup grated Parmesan cheese
- Salt and freshly ground black pepper to taste

Place all the ingredients in a food processor or blender and process until smooth, scraping the sides of the bowl frequently.

Broccoli Pesto Snails

Makes 32

Here's an inventive yet easy way to showcase your Broccoli Pesto. Make these ahead and store them in the freezer for a handy appetizer or snack.

    1 package Pillsbury Crescent rolls
    ½ cup Broccoli Pesto (page 23)

Preheat the oven to 375°F with the rack in the upper third, but not highest, position. Line a heavy-duty baking sheet with aluminum foil or spray it with nonstick vegetable cooking oil.

Unwrap the dough and gently roll it with a rolling pin to make the perforated lines disappear. Cut the dough into four equal squares and spread each piece with 2 tablespoons of pesto.

Roll each piece into a compact roll and then use a sharp knife to cut each roll into eight pieces. Transfer the pieces to the prepared baking sheet, cut sides up and down, and bake for 10 to 12 minutes or until the dough is puffed and golden brown and the filling bubbly. Serve immediately.

Broccoli Pesto–Stuffed Mushrooms

Makes about 20

Stuff button mushroom caps with Broccoli Pesto for a delicious, easy finger food.

20 large white or golden mushrooms, as close to the same size as possible

¾ cup Broccoli Pesto (page 23)

Preheat the oven to 375°F. Line a baking sheet with aluminum foil, brush it with olive oil, or spray it with nonstick vegetable cooking oil. Clean the mushrooms either by wiping them with a damp paper towel or briefly washing them, then patting them dry. Twist off the stems, trim the very ends, and discard the ends.

Chop the mushroom stems and mix into the pesto. Invert the caps and fill each with a generous tablespoon of pesto. Press the filling into the cap, rounding the top.

Place the caps on the prepared baking sheet and bake for 15 minutes. Serve hot or at room temperature.

Prosciutto Roll-ups

Makes about 18

This recipe was inspired by the 1960s cocktail-party standby of cream cheese–ham pinwheels. This version is an appetizer-in-a-jiffy with a modern taste. Make these several hours ahead, cover with plastic wrap, and refrigerate until serving time.

⅓ pound prosciutto, thinly sliced

½ cup Broccoli Pesto (page 23)

Spread each slice of prosciutto with a thin layer of pesto. Roll up each slice tightly, starting from the narrow end. Use a sharp knife to slice each roll into 1-inch long pieces (cutting them on the diagonal makes them even prettier). Place on a platter and serve.

Broccoli Roquefort Tart

Makes 9 three-inch squares

Serve this as a brunch dish, a luncheon main course, or as a first course before a light supper. You can substitute Stilton or blue cheese for the Roquefort.

One 17 1/4-ounce package frozen puff pastry, defrosted according to package directions

2/3 cup thinly sliced celery

2 cups broccoli florets, cut into small clusters and steamed or microwaved for 2 minutes

6 ounces Roquefort cheese, crumbled

1/3 cup sour cream or nonfat sour cream

1/3 cup mayonnaise or light mayonnaise

1 large egg

Preheat the oven to 350°F.

Place one sheet of puff pastry on an ungreased baking sheet. Cut four 1/2-inch-wide strips from a second sheet of pastry. Form the edges of the tart by moistening the edges of the first sheet and placing the cut-out strips to frame the edges. Trim as necessary. Press down lightly to seal the edges.

Distribute the celery and broccoli inside the edges of the tart. Scatter the cheese over the top.

Mix together the sour cream, mayonnaise, and egg. Pour this mixture over the vegetables and cheese.

Bake for 30 to 40 minutes or until the pastry is golden brown.

Broccoli in Phyllo

Serves 8 to 10

Spanakopita is a savory Greek pastry traditionally made with spinach. This version makes one large pastry that is stuffed with broccoli and feta cheese. A smashing luncheon dish or a spectacular first course for a fancy dinner, it can be made up to eight hours ahead of time and refrigerated until ready to cook.

- 1 tablespoon olive oil
- ½ cup finely chopped onions
- 1 clove garlic, chopped
- 5 cups broccoli stems, peeled, steamed or microwaved for 2 minutes or until just tender, drained, and then coarsely chopped
- 8 ounces feta cheese, crumbled
- 1 cup cottage cheese (you may substitute low- or nonfat versions)
- 4 large eggs, lightly beaten
- ¾ cup black olives, pitted and coarsely chopped (if you can find Greek oil-cured olives, use them)
- 1 stick (4 ounces) butter or margarine
- ½ cup olive oil
- 1 pound frozen phyllo dough, thawed according to package directions

Preheat the oven to 350°F with the rack in the center position. Line a baking sheet with aluminum foil or spray it with nonstick vegetable cooking oil.

Heat the oil in a small skillet and sauté the onions and garlic until translucent. Transfer to a large bowl. Add the broccoli, feta and cottage cheeses, eggs, and olives. Stir gently to combine the ingredients. Set aside.

In the same skillet, melt the butter together with the olive oil.

Remove the sheets of phyllo one at a time. Place the first sheet in the center of the baking sheet and brush it with melted butter and oil. Place the next sheet obliquely 1 inch to the first sheet. Oil this sheet too. Continue rotating the sheets and oiling until you have all the sheets of phyllo stacked up.

Place the filling in the center of the oiled sheets and draw up the edges to the center. Squeeze together the edges in the center but don't seal them tightly as you want the phyllo to open up slightly while baking. Press gently on the sides until you have a nicely rounded shape.

Bake for 1 hour and 15 minutes. The phyllo should be a beautiful golden color and the filling should be set (a knife inserted will come out clean). It is important to let the pouch sit 15 minutes to firm up and absorb any juices. (It can sit longer as it will stay warm a long time.)

Slide the phyllo onto a serving plate and cut it into wedges to serve.

Broccoli and Cheese in Puff Pastry

Makes 18

Frozen puff pastry, available in your supermarket, makes this elegant appetizer a snap to prepare. It will look as if you've cooked all day. However, you can put these turnovers together up to eight hours ahead, refrigerate, and then bake them just before serving.

- 1 cup crumbled feta, goat, Stilton, or Roquefort cheese
- 1 extra-large egg
- 2 cups broccoli stems and florets, stems peeled, steamed or microwaved for 2 minutes until just tender, drained, and then chopped into 1/2-inch pieces
- 1/4 teaspoon freshly ground black pepper
- One 17 1/4-ounce package frozen puff pastry, defrosted according to package directions
- 1 egg white beaten with 1 teaspoon cold water

Preheat the oven to 350°F with the rack in the center position. Line a heavy-duty baking sheet with aluminum foil.

In a bowl, combine the cheese, egg, broccoli, and pepper. Mix well to combine.

Unroll the puff pastry and cut each sheet into nine squares. Refrigerate the squares, removing two at a time from the refrigerator as you assemble them. Use a rolling pin to roll each piece into a 4-inch square. Place 1 tablespoon of filling in the center of each square, moisten the edges with a little water and fold over one corner to meet the opposite corner. Press the seams with a fork to seal the edges shut, then transfer to the prepared baking sheet. Use a small knife to cut a ½-inch vent in the top of each turnover. Brush the egg mixture over the top of each turnover.

Bake for 20 minutes or until the pastry is puffed and golden brown. Serve hot.

BROCCOLI
Salads

Curried Broccoli Potato Salad

Serves 6

This can be either a vegetarian side dish or an entrée with the addition of cubed smoked turkey, ham, or even tofu. This can be made ahead up to twenty-four hours and stored in a covered container in the refrigerator.

- 4 medium-sized boiling potatoes, well scrubbed, peeled, and cut into 8 pieces
- 1/2 cup mayonnaise, light mayonnaise, or low-fat yogurt
- 1 teaspoon curry powder
- 2 cups broccoli stems and florets, stems peeled, steamed or microwaved for 2 minutes or until just tender
- 1/3 cup golden raisins
- 1 cup cubed smoked turkey, ham, or tofu (optional)
- 1/4 cup roasted cashew halves

Place the potatoes in water to cover in a large saucepan. Bring to a boil, lower the heat, and simmer for about 15 minutes or until tender when pierced with a fork. Drain, cool, and slice into 1-inch pieces. Place in a bowl and set aside.

Mix together the mayonnaise and curry powder. Add to the potatoes.

Add the broccoli and raisins and toss until well mixed, being careful not to break the potatoes. Add the turkey, if desired.

Spoon into a serving bowl and garnish with the cashews.

Tortellini and Broccoli Salad

Serves 6 as a first course

Making your own version of this fancy takeout specialty salad will save you an amazing amount of money. If you can't find sun-dried tomatoes packed in oil, you can make your own by rinsing sun-dried tomatoes in white vinegar to remove some of the salt, placing them in a glass jar, and covering them with extra-virgin olive oil. They will be softened and ready to use the next day.

1½ cups broccoli stems and florets, stems peeled, steamed or microwaved 2 minutes or until just tender, drained, and cut into 1-inch pieces

½ pound frozen or dried cheese-filled tortellini

3 tablespoons red wine vinegar

⅓ cup olive oil from the sun-dried tomatoes

1 teaspoon Dijon mustard

8 oil-packed sun-dried tomatoes, quartered

2 anchovy filets, coarsely chopped (optional)

2 tablespoons pine nuts

¼ teaspoon freshly ground black pepper

1 cup spinach, well rinsed, stems removed, torn into bite-sized pieces, and firmly packed

1 small head Boston lettuce, torn into bite-sized pieces

Cook the tortellini according to package directions. Rinse briefly with cold water, then drain well.

To make the dressing, combine the vinegar, oil, mustard, tomatoes, anchovies, pine nuts, and pepper in a mixing bowl.

Place the spinach and lettuce in the bottom of a salad bowl or on a serving platter. Combine the tortellini and broccoli, toss with the dressing, and place in the center of the greens.

Broccoli Tuna Fish

Serves 4

Here's a new twist on an old classic. The addition of capers and Italian canned tuna give it a changed personality. Try serving this over slices of toasted Italian bread.

One 7-ounce can Italian tuna, packed in oil
1 cup broccoli stems and florets, stems peeled, chopped into small pieces
1 small onion, minced
1 tablespoon capers, drained
Juice of 1 lemon

Place the tuna with its oil in a bowl. Add all the remaining ingredients and stir well to mix.

Broccoli Bean Salad

Serves 8

The addition of fresh herbs gives this dish a lovely taste that is well complemented by the combination of textures. It's even better made the day before and refrigerated overnight in a covered container. This gives the flavors a chance to meld.

One 19-ounce can red kidney beans, rinsed and drained

One 19-ounce can white kidney beans, rinsed and drained

2 cups small broccoli florets, steamed or microwaved for 2 minutes or until just tender

⅓ cup chopped red onions

1 small green bell pepper, cored, seeded, and coarsely chopped

1 clove garlic, minced

½ cup olive oil

3 to 4 tablespoons red wine vinegar

1 tablespoon chopped fresh oregano, or 1 teaspoon dried oregano

4 large fresh basil leaves, chopped, or 1 teaspoon dried basil

½ teaspoon salt

Pinch of freshly ground black pepper

In a bowl, combine the beans, broccoli, onions, and peppers.

In another bowl, mix together the garlic, oil, vinegar, oregano, basil, salt, and pepper.

Pour the dressing over the vegetables and either serve immediately or refrigerate overnight in a covered container.

Lebanese Broccoli Salad

Serves 12

Here is another simple make-ahead salad that will keep for up to a week in a covered container in your refrigerator. If you cannot find fresh mint, you may substitute dried. You may chop the ingredients in the food processor, but take care not to turn them into mush.

- 1 cup bulgur, soaked in 1 cup boiling water for 30 minutes and then drained
- 2 cups firmly packed Italian (flat-leaf) parsley, leaves only, chopped
- 1 cup fresh mint leaves, chopped, or 4 tablespoons dried mint
- 3 cups broccoli stems, peeled, steamed, or microwaved for 2 minutes or until just tender, and cut into ½-inch pieces
- 1 large tomato, chopped
- One 19-ounce can chick-peas, well rinsed and drained
- ¼ cup fresh lemon juice
- ⅓ cup olive oil
- 2 cloves garlic, minced
- Salt and freshly ground black pepper to taste

In a bowl, combine the bulgur, parsley, mint, broccoli, tomatoes, and chick-peas.

In another bowl, combine the lemon juice, oil, and garlic. Stir to mix well and pour over the vegetable mixture. Season with salt and pepper to taste.

Hot Broccoli Salad

Serves 4

This Oriental-style stir-fry takes only minutes to prepare. You can turn it into an entrée by adding stir-fried strips of boneless chicken or beef.

- 1 tablespoon soy sauce
- 1 teaspoon dry sherry
- 1 teaspoon sugar
- 1 tablespoon vegetable oil
- 1 tablespoon sesame oil
- 2 cups broccoli stems and florets, stems peeled and cut into 2-inch pieces
- 2 cups thinly sliced Chinese cabbage
- 1 cup sliced water chestnuts, well rinsed and drained
- 2 tablespoons sesame seeds

Combine the soy sauce, sherry, and sugar in a bowl and set aside.

Heat the oils in a wok or large skillet. Add the vegetables and quickly stir-fry, cooking only until the cabbage starts to wilt, about 2 minutes.

Remove the vegetables to a serving dish. Add the sauce and mix well. Sprinkle on the sesame seeds and serve immediately.

Wheat Berry Salad

Serves 6

Wheat berries are available in health food stores. They add a satisfying crunch to this easy-to-prepare salad. However, remember that wheat berries must be soaked overnight before you prepare this dish. And if you are not able to find Jerusalem artichokes, you can substitute more broccoli.

- 1 cup wheat berries, soaked overnight in 2 cups boiling water, drained
- 1 scallion, green and white parts, chopped
- 2 stalks celery, thinly sliced (1 cup)
- 2 fresh Jerusalem artichokes, washed, peeled, and thinly sliced (about 1/2 cup)
- 1 cup broccoli stems and florets, stems peeled and cut crosswise into thin slices
- 3/4 cup plain yogurt
- 1 medium onion, thinly sliced
- 1 tablespoon soy sauce
- 1/2 teaspoon freshly ground black pepper
- 1/4 cup fresh dill, chopped

In a bowl, combine the softened wheat berries, scallions, celery, artichokes, and broccoli.

In another bowl, mix together the yogurt, onions, soy sauce, pepper, and dill. Toss the dressing with the salad and serve.

Broccoli and Water Chestnut Salad

Serves 6

Fresh ginger adds a zing to this Oriental-flavored salad.

3 cups broccoli florets, separated, steamed, or microwaved for 2 minutes or until just tender

One 8-ounce can sliced water chestnuts, rinsed and drained

⅓ C   2 tablespoons red wine vinegar

I C   ⅓ cup olive oil

I T   1 teaspoon sesame oil + +

2 T   2 teaspoons soy sauce

2 T   1 tablespoon fresh ginger, peeled and cut in thin slivers

1 small head romaine lettuce

1 small head Boston lettuce

4 +   2 tablespoons toasted sesame seeds (see Note)

In a bowl, combine the broccoli and water chestnuts.

In another bowl, mix together the vinegar, oils, soy sauce, and ginger. Pour this dressing over the broccoli.

Tear the lettuce into 3-inch pieces and use it to line a serving bowl. Pile the broccoli mixture in the center and sprinkle with the sesame seeds.

NOTE: To toast sesame seeds, place the seeds in a small skillet over high heat. Stir constantly or shake the pan rapidly back and forth, moving the seeds until they are golden brown and you can smell the rich sesame aroma.

7/20/07

Broccoli Orange Salad

Serves 8

The addition of dried fruits and nuts makes for an unusually delicious blend of flavors and textures.

- 3 cups broccoli stems and florets, stems peeled, sliced into 1-inch pieces on the diagonal, and steamed or microwaved for 2 minutes or until just tender
- 1 large seedless orange, zest grated, fruit cut into 1-inch chunks
- 2 tablespoons honey
- ¼ cup fresh orange juice
- 2 tablespoons vegetable oil
- 1 teaspoon cider vinegar
- ¼ teaspoon dry mustard
- 1 teaspoon soy sauce
- 1 cup bean sprouts
- ⅓ cup dried apricots, quartered
- ½ cup slivered almonds

In a serving bowl, combine the broccoli, orange, and orange zest.

In another bowl, mix together the honey, orange juice, oil, vinegar, mustard, and soy sauce. Pour the dressing over the broccoli.

Add the sprouts, apricots, and almonds. Cover and refrigerate for 30 minutes before serving.

Broccoli-Pear-Roquefort Salad

Serves 4

Try serving this beautiful salad arranged on individual serving plates. If you cannot find Roquefort cheese, you can substitute Stilton or blue cheese. Sprinkle lemon juice on the pear slices right after cutting them to keep them from turning brown.

- 1 bunch watercress, tough stems removed, leaves rinsed and patted dry
- 2 firm Bartlett pears, sliced lengthwise in quarters, cored and stemmed, then thinly sliced
- 2 cups broccoli florets, steamed or microwaved for 2 minutes or until just tender, rinsed under cold water and drained
- 2 scallions, white part only, finely chopped
- 1 cup thinly sliced (on the diagonal) celery
- ½ cup walnuts, coarsely chopped
- ⅓ cup Roquefort cheese, crumbled
- ½ cup plain yogurt, or ½ cup mayonnaise

Dash of hot sauce to taste

Divide the watercress among four salad plates. Arrange the pear slices and broccoli over the watercress. Top with scallions, celery, and walnuts.

In a bowl, mix together the cheese and yogurt. Add hot sauce to taste. Spoon the dressing over the salad and serve immediately.

Broccoli and Feta Salad

Serves 6

Here is a broccoli version of a classic Greek salad. The optional addition of sardines (or canned tuna, if you prefer) makes this suitable for a luncheon dish or light supper entrée.

- 3 cups broccoli florets, steamed or microwaved for 2 minutes or until just tender, drained, cooled, and cut into 1-inch pieces
- 2 Italian plum tomatoes, cut into 1/4-inch slices
- 1 cup sliced fresh mushrooms
- 1/3 cup feta cheese, crumbled
- 4 sardines, chopped, or one 14-ounce can tuna, drained
- 1 Bermuda onion, thinly sliced, separated into rings
- 1/4 cup olive oil
- 2 tablespoons red wine vinegar
- 1 teaspoon Dijon mustard

Freshly ground black pepper to taste

In a serving bowl, toss together the broccoli, tomatoes, and mushrooms. Gently mix in the feta, sardines, and onions.

In another bowl, mix together the oil, vinegar, mustard, and pepper. Pour over the salad and toss just before serving.

BROCCOLI
with Other Vegetables

Broccoli Rice Casserole

Serves 6 to 8

A great dish for a pot luck supper: It's easy to make ahead (up to twenty-four hours) and can be reheated either in a microwave or in a conventional oven.

- 1 cup long-grain white rice
- 2 cups chicken broth, or 2 chicken or vegetable bouillon cubes dissolved in 2 cups hot water
- 2 tablespoons butter or margarine
- 1 medium onion, coarsely chopped
- 4 cups broccoli stems and florets, stems peeled and cut into bite-sized pieces
- ½ cup grated Parmesan cheese

Cook the rice in the microwave by combining the rice, broth, and butter in a 2-quart microwavable container. Cover with plastic wrap and microwave on high for 12 to 14 minutes. Or cook in a pan with broth and butter on the stove top according to package directions.

Preheat the oven to 350°F with the rack in the center position. Grease or spray with nonstick vegetable cooking oil a 2-quart casserole.

Place a layer of cooked rice on the bottom of the casserole, top with half of the broccoli, half of the onion, and half of the cheese. Repeat this, ending with the cheese.

Bake, loosely covered with aluminum foil, for 20 minutes or until a knife inserted in the center comes out hot. You can also microwave this dish, covered with plastic wrap, on high power for 5 minutes.

Broccoli-Stuffed Cabbage

Serves 8

This is a new take on an Old World recipe. You will be amazed at how easy this is to make when you don't have to cook the cabbage ahead of time. This dish freezes beautifully, so make extra to have some for another time.

> 1 medium head cabbage
>
> 2 teaspoons olive oil
>
> 1 large onion, coarsely chopped
>
> 1 pound lean ground beef or turkey
>
> 1 cup chopped broccoli stems and florets, stems peeled
>
> 1 cup cooked white or brown rice
>
> ½ teaspoon salt
>
> ¼ teaspoon freshly ground black pepper
>
> 1 large onion, chopped
>
> 2 cloves garlic, minced
>
> One 28-ounce can whole tomatoes with puree
>
> One 15-ounce can tomato sauce
>
> 3 tablespoons brown sugar
>
> ½ cup raisins

Three hours before you plan to make this dish, cut the stem end off the cabbage and place the cabbage in the freezer for 2 hours. Remove it to a work space and let the cabbage defrost for 1 hour. The leaves will have wilted and are ready to wrap around the filling.

Or, you can use the more traditional method: Heat a large pot of boiling water. Cut the core from cabbage and separate the leaves, trimming as needed. Drop the cabbage leaves, four at a time, into the boiling water and remove them with tongs as each leaf becomes wilted and pliable.

Heat the oil in a large frying pan over medium-high heat. Sauté one onion until tender. Add the ground meat and cook until well done. Drain. Add the broccoli, rice, salt, and pepper. Mix well.

In a bowl, combine the other onion , garlic, tomatoes, tomato sauce, brown sugar, and raisins.

Preheat the oven to 350°F with the rack in the center position. Spray a 9-inch × 13-inch baking dish with nonstick vegetable cooking spray.

Place ½ cup of the tomato sauce on the bottom of the baking dish.

Lay the cabbage leaves flat, with the stem end facing you. Place 2 heaping tablespoons of the filling in the center of each leaf. Fold the stem end of the leaf over the filling. Fold in each side. Roll up into neat little bundles. Place the rolls in the baking dish, seam side down.

Pour the rest of the sauce over the rolls and bake for 30 minutes.

Broccoli and Shiitake Mushrooms with Udon

Serves 4

Udon noodles, available in both supermarkets and health food stores, are a Japanese product made from wheat flour. Dried shiitake mushrooms are usually available in specialty produce shops and sometimes in the supermarket.

- ½ cup dried shiitake mushrooms, soaked in warm water for 30 minutes, drained
- 1 tablespoon vegetable oil
- 3 cups broccoli florets, cut into bite-sized pieces
- ½ large red bell pepper, cored, seeded, and cut into thin strips
- 3 tablespoons water
- One 14-ounce package dried Japanese udon noodles
- 3 tablespoons vegetable oil
- ¼ cup soy sauce
- ⅓ cup water
- 3 tablespoons oyster sauce

Slice the shiitake mushrooms in thin strips. Set aside.

Boil a large pot of water for the noodles.

Place the wok over medium-high heat. Add the 1 tablespoon of oil and heat. Add the broccoli and red peppers and stir-fry until well coated with oil and slightly tender, about 2 to 3 minutes.

Sprinkle the 3 tablespoons water around the edges of the wok. Cover and steam the mixture for 3 minutes or until tender.

Cook the noodles according to package directions, drain well, and place in a serving dish. Add the broccoli and peppers.

Add the 3 tablespoons of oil to the wok and, over moderate heat, stir-fry the mushrooms for 1 minute. Add the soy sauce, oyster sauce, and 1/3 cup water to the wok and stir well, scraping down the sides of the wok.

Pour the mushrooms and sauce over the vegetables and noodles. Toss to combine all the ingredients and serve at once.

Broccoli and Beautiful Mushrooms

Serves 8

A show dish filled with elegant ingredients. Look for enoki and shiitake mushrooms in your supermarket or in food shops that specialize in fresh produce. If you cannot find them, use more of the white mushrooms or others such as oyster or portobello mushrooms.

4 cups broccoli florets, cut into bite-sized pieces, steamed or microwaved for 2 minutes or until just tender

8 ounces white mushrooms, cleaned and sliced

3 ounces enoki mushrooms

3 ounces shiitake mushrooms, cleaned, stems trimmed, and sliced

2½ tablespoons fresh lemon juice

1 tablespoon honey

2 tablespoons vegetable oil

1 teaspoon grated lemon peel

1 tablespoon finely chopped onions

Put the broccoli in a serving bowl and top with the white mushrooms. Toss gently to avoid breaking the mushrooms. Scatter the enoki and shiitake mushrooms on top.

Mix together the lemon juice, honey, oil, lemon peel, and onions and pour this mixture over the broccoli and mushrooms.

Serve as a hot first course or as a side dish with fish or chicken.

Chick-peas and Broccoli with Lemon Pepper

Serves 6

This makes a great brown-bag lunch when stuffed into a pita pocket. It will keep for up to one week in a covered container in the refrigerator. Look for lemon pepper in the seasoning section of your supermarket.

3 cups broccoli florets, steamed or microwaved for 2 minutes or until just tender

One 19-ounce can chick-peas, drained

1/4 cup fresh lemon juice

1/4 cup olive oil

Grated rind of 1 lemon

1/4 to 1/2 teaspoon lemon pepper

Toss the broccoli and chick-peas together in a serving bowl.

Mix together the lemon juice, oil, lemon rind, and pepper. Toss with the broccoli and chick-peas and serve.

Broccoli
with Snow Peas

Serves 8

Toasted sesame seeds give a wonderfully aromatic crunch to this dish. It's best to use fresh snow peas rather than frozen.

- 2 tablespoons sesame seeds
- 4 cups broccoli florets, steamed or microwaved for 2 minutes or until just tender
- 2 cups snow peas, ends and strings removed, steamed or microwaved for 1 minute
- 1 tablespoon vegetable oil
- 1 teaspoon sesame oil
- 1 teaspoon fresh lemon juice
- 1 tablespoon soy sauce

Toast the sesame seeds in a dry nonstick skillet set over medium-high heat, shaking the pan briskly to agitate the seeds until they turn a deep tan, about 4 to 5 minutes.

Combine the broccoli and snow peas in a serving bowl. Sprinkle with sesame seeds.

Mix together the oils, lemon juice, and soy sauce and drizzle over the vegetables. Serve at once.

Broccoli-Stuffed Acorn Squash

Serves 4

Acorn squash are abundant in the fall. This recipe is a perfect vegetarian dish: Make with large squash for a delicious entrée or with smaller squash for a side dish.

- 2 medium acorn squash
- 2 tablespoons water
- 2 cups broccoli florets, cut into bite-sized pieces and steamed or microwaved for 2 minutes or until just tender
- 1/4 cup fresh orange juice
- 2 tablespoons dark brown sugar
- 1 tablespoon butter or margarine, melted

Cut the squash in half lengthwise and scoop out the seeds. Place the squash, cut sides down, on a plate. Sprinkle the tops with water, cover with plastic wrap, and microwave for 5 minutes. Or place the squash, cut sides down, in a baking dish, sprinkle with water, and bake at 350°F for 45 minutes.

Divide the broccoli among the squash halves. Mix together the orange juice, brown sugar, and butter and drizzle over the broccoli.

Cover with plastic wrap and microwave for 8 to 10 minutes or until the squash is tender when pierced with a fork. Or return the squash to the baking dish and bake at 350°F for 15 more minutes.

Broccoli
and Spaghetti Squash
Serves 6

Vidalia onions are readily available in the spring. They are prized for their taste, which is so sweet you can eat them like a piece of fruit. If you cannot find Vidalia onions, you can substitute Spanish onions. The combination of colors here—bright yellow squash and the deep green of the broccoli—makes this a visually stunning dish.

1 large (2 to 3 pounds) spaghetti squash

3 tablespoons water

1 tablespoon olive oil

1 medium sweet Spanish or Vidalia onion, thinly sliced

1 clove garlic, minced

1 small zucchini, thinly sliced

3 cups broccoli stems and florets, stems peeled and thinly sliced on the diagonal

2 tablespoons water

1 scallion, green and white parts, chopped

Cut the spaghetti squash in half lengthwise. Scoop out the seeds and invert the squash halves on a plate. Sprinkle with the 3 tablespoons water, cover with plastic wrap, and microwave for 5 to 7 minutes. Or invert the halves in a shallow aluminum foil–lined baking pan with water and bake at 350°F for 45 minutes. The skin should be tender when pricked with a fork. Cool slightly.

Heat the oil in a skillet over medium-high heat and sauté the onions and garlic until just tender and transparent but not browned. Add the zucchini and broccoli and the 2 tablespoons water. Cover and steam over medium heat for 2 to 3 minutes until the broccoli is crisp-tender. Remove the pan from the heat.

Gently separate the spaghetti strings from the squash by scraping the insides of the squash with a fork. Remove them to a serving bowl and gently mix with the other vegetables. Garnish with scallions and serve.

Broccoli and Chayote

Serves 4

Chayote is a flattish, light green, gourd-shaped fruit grown in South America and Mexico that has gained popularity in the United States because of its versatility and mild flavor. Look for these especially during the winter months in Spanish markets and in your supermarket as well.

1 chayote, about 4 inches by 5 inches

1 tablespoon butter or margarine

3 tablespoons sliced almonds

2 cups coarsely chopped broccoli florets, steamed or microwaved for 2 minutes or until just tender

Place the chayote in a small saucepan. Cover with water and boil for 15 to 20 minutes or until the skin pierces easily with a fork. Drain, cool slightly, and peel. Cut the chayote in half, remove and discard the seed, and cut the chayote lengthwise in thin slices.

Melt the butter over medium heat in a small pan. Add the almonds and sauté until the almonds begin to turn golden. Remove the pan from the heat immediately.

Gently toss together the chayote and broccoli in a serving bowl. Garnish with almonds and serve.

Broccoli-Tomato Casserole

Serves 8

While this recipe calls for cherry tomatoes, you may substitute beefsteak tomatoes when they are in season. This casserole can be assembled up to eight hours ahead, refrigerated, and then baked just before serving.

6 cups broccoli stems and florets, stems peeled, cut into bite-sized pieces, steamed or microwaved for 2 minutes or until just tender

1 cup cherry tomatoes, halved, or beefsteak tomatoes, cut into 1-inch slices

4 tablespoons butter or margarine

2 tablespoons all-purpose flour

1 cup whole, low-fat, or skim milk

3 tablespoons grated Parmesan cheese

Preheat the oven to 350°F. Spray a 2-quart casserole with nonstick vegetable cooking oil. Add the broccoli and tomatoes to the casserole.

Melt the butter in a small, heavy-bottomed saucepan. Sprinkle on the flour and cook over moderate heat, stirring constantly, for 5 minutes. Slowly add the milk and continue cooking until thickened, about 5 minutes. Pour the mixture over the casserole. Sprinkle with cheese.

Bake for 30 minutes or until the top is brown and the sauce bubbly.

Broccoli-Stuffed Parmesan Tomatoes

Serves 4

If possible, wait for ripe summer tomatoes to make this dish. Select tomatoes that are as close to the same size as possible so they will cook in about the same amount of time.

- 4 large ripe tomatoes
- 2 cups broccoli stems and florets, stems peeled and cut into ½-inch pieces
- 1 small onion, chopped
- ¼ cup fresh basil, chopped
- ¼ teaspoon freshly ground black pepper
- Salt to taste
- ⅓ cup olive oil
- ½ cup grated Parmesan cheese

Preheat the oven to 350°F. Spray a 9-inch square baking dish with nonstick vegetable cooking oil.

If the tomatoes are wobbly and won't sit flat in the dish, trim a thin slice off the bottom. With a serrated knife, slice off the top ½ inch of the tomatoes and use a grapefruit spoon to gently scoop out the seeds and some of the pulp. Chop the scooped-out part and reserve.

In a bowl, combine the chopped tomatoes, broccoli, onions, basil, pepper, and salt. Divide this filling among the tomatoes and push it gently into the cavities. Drizzle with olive oil and top with grated cheese.

Place the tomatoes in the baking dish and bake for 20 to 30 minutes, depending on the size of your tomatoes. The tomatoes are ready when the cheese is brown and the tomatoes look soft but have not fallen apart.

Spicy Tomato and Broccoli

Serves 8

You can use broccoli rape (Italian broccoli) in this recipe, if you wish. If you have a pepper grinder, this is the time to use it. Freshly ground black pepper adds zest to this dish.

    1 tablespoon olive oil
    1 cup chopped onions
    One 8-ounce can whole Italian tomatoes with juices
    ½ pound Romano cheese, cut into ¼-inch cubes
    1 teaspoon freshly ground black pepper
    1 large bunch broccoli (about 1 pound), cut into
        medium spears, stems peeled, or broccoli rape,
        large outer leaves removed
    5 to 8 drops hot sauce (optional)

Heat the oil in a large skillet over medium-high heat. Add the onions and cook until tender. Add the tomatoes, cheese, and pepper and bring to a boil.

Reduce the heat to medium, add the broccoli, and cook, covered, for about 5 minutes or until the broccoli is very tender. Sprinkle on hot sauce and serve immediately.

Fast Broccoli-Tomato Pasta Sauce

Serves 6

Whenever possible, use fresh herbs to complement this dish. You can serve it as a main course or as a substantial appetizer before a light entrée.

- **2** teaspoons olive oil
- **½** cup chopped onions
- **½** cup cored, seeded, and chopped green bell peppers
- **2** cloves garlic, minced
- **One** 28-ounce can crushed tomatoes
- **¼** cup chopped fresh oregano
- **½** cup chopped fresh basil
- **½** cup dry white wine
- **1** pound spaghetti (for variety, use tomato or red pepper pasta)
- **4** cups broccoli florets, cut into bite-sized pieces

Heat the oil in a skillet over medium-high heat. Add the onions, peppers, and garlic and sauté until just tender. Lower the heat to medium and add the tomatoes, herbs, and wine. Simmer for 20 minutes.

Cook the spaghetti according to package directions until al dente. Drain well.

Add the broccoli florets to the tomato sauce and simmer, covered, until the broccoli is tender and still crisp, about 4 minutes.

Serve the broccoli-tomato sauce over the pasta.

Broccoli and Carrot Matchsticks

Serves 4

The inner stems of the broccoli are sweet and tender when the outer skins are removed. You can even eat them raw as a low-calorie high-vitamin snack. In this dish, the pieces are briefly steamed and combined with carrots and fresh mint.

- 1 cup broccoli stems, peeled and cut into matchsticks
- 1 cup carrots, peeled and cut into matchsticks
- 1 tablespoon sweet (unsalted) butter, melted
- 1 tablespoon dark brown sugar
- 1 tablespoon fresh lemon juice
- 1/4 cup chopped fresh mint
- Salt to taste

Steam or microwave the broccoli and carrots together for 2 minutes or until just tender. Rinse under cold water, drain well, and place in a serving dish.

In a bowl, mix together the butter, brown sugar, and lemon juice. Pour over the vegetables, add the mint, and adjust the seasoning. Toss together and serve.

Broccoli with Baby Carrots in Brown Butter Sauce

Serves 6 to 8

Keep a careful eye on the butter while you brown it. It can turn from golden brown to burned in a very few seconds. The pleasant nutty taste of the browned butter adds a delicate flavor to the vegetables.

One 12-ounce package baby carrots, ready to cook

3 to 4 cups broccoli florets with 2-inch stems, separated into thin spears

3 tablespoons butter

2 teaspoons fresh lemon juice

Salt and freshly ground black pepper to taste

Place a steamer rack in the bottom of a large pot. Add 1 inch of water and bring to a simmer. Place the carrots on the rack and steam, covered, for 5 minutes. Add the broccoli on top of the carrots and steam for an additional 2 minutes. The carrots should be just tender. Remove the vegetables to a serving dish.

Heat the butter in a heavy skillet over moderate heat. Watch carefully while the butter sizzles. As soon as it begins to turn brown, remove it from the heat, let cool for 2 to 3 minutes, and add the lemon juice (take care not to splatter hot butter on yourself).

Pour the butter sauce over the vegetables, season with salt and pepper, and serve.

Oven-Roasted Potatoes and Broccoli

Serves 6

Roasting the vegetables in the oven at high heat gives them a wonderful crunchy crust. You can make a meal of this dish by adding a loaf of crusty bread and some goat cheese.

⅓ cup olive oil

1 bunch broccoli (about 1 pound), stems peeled and cut into 4-inch × 1-inch pieces

8 red bliss potatoes (2 to 3 inches each), scrubbed and quartered

1 large Spanish onion, cut into 1-inch-thick slices, rings separated

2 tablespoons chopped fresh rosemary, or 2 teaspoons dried rosemary

Salt and freshly ground black pepper to taste

Preheat the oven to 450°F with the rack in the upper position.

Pour the oil into a roasting pan. Add the broccoli, potatoes, and onions. Toss well to cover with the oil, adding more if necessary to coat all the vegetables. Place the pan, uncovered, in the oven and roast for 15 minutes, tossing the vegetables with a slotted spoon twice during the cooking time.

Add the rosemary and cook for an additional 5 to 7 minutes or until the potatoes are tender when pierced with a fork, and the onions and broccoli are beginning to look crisp and brown. Season with salt and pepper to taste before serving.

Broccoli-Stuffed Vidalias

Serves 4

If you can find the sweet Vidalia onions available in the early spring, use them to make this dish. If not, use Spanish onions, which are also mild but not as sweet.

- 4 sweet Vidalia or Spanish onions
- 1½ cups broccoli stems, peeled and chopped into ½-inch pieces
- ¾ cup plain bread crumbs
- 1 tablespoon chopped fresh tarragon, or ½ teaspoon dried tarragon
- 1 tablespoon chopped fresh rosemary, or ½ teaspoon dried rosemary
- 2 tablespoons coarsely chopped sun-dried tomatoes packed in oil, drained
- 2 tablespoons melted butter or margarine
- 4 ounces herbed, peppered, or plain goat cheese
- ¾ cup white wine
- 4 tablespoons olive oil

Preheat the oven to 375°F.

Peel the onions and scoop out a ¾-inch indentation in the top of each onion using a grapefruit spoon or small paring knife. Reserve the pieces you scoop out, chop them and measure ½ cup, and set aside. Trim the root ends of the onions so that they will sit flat and place the onions in a flat baking dish sprayed with non-stick vegetable cooking oil.

Mix together the broccoli, bread crumbs, reserved chopped onions, herbs, tomatoes, and butter. Pile the mixture into the cavities of the onions.

Slice the goat cheese into four pieces and place one piece, flat side down, on top of each of the stuffed onions. Pour the wine over all. Drizzle each onion with 1 tablespoon olive oil. Bake, basting with juices once or twice during the baking, for 45 minutes or until the onions are tender when pricked with a fork and the cheese is browned.

Feta and Broccoli–Stuffed Potatoes

Serves 4

This is a meal in minutes, especially if you use the microwave to bake the potatoes. You can substitute cottage cheese (regular or low-fat) for the feta, if you wish.

    4 medium Idaho potatoes, baked
    3 tablespoons butter or margarine
    ½ cup crumbled feta cheese
    2 cups broccoli florets, cut into ½-inch clusters
    2 tablespoons grated Parmesan cheese

Preheat the oven to 375°F with the rack in the center position.

Lay the warm potatoes on a flat surface and slit open the tops lengthwise.

Scoop out most of the insides of the potatoes, leaving about ½ inch on the sides to form a solid bowl shape. Add the insides of the potatoes to a bowl.

Add the butter to the potatoes in the bowl and mash together with a fork. Gently mix in the feta cheese and broccoli.

Pile the broccoli mixture in the scooped out potato halves. Sprinkle with Parmesan cheese. Place the potatoes in a baking dish and bake for 10 minutes. Serve hot or at room temperature.

Broccoli, Onions, and Roasted Red Peppers

Serves 8 to 10

This dish makes a splendid addition to a holiday table and is the perfect accompaniment to roast turkey, baked ham, or roast beef. Prepare all the vegetables up to eight hours ahead and do the cooking at the last minute.

- 1 pound small white onions, root ends trimmed
- ½ cup cider vinegar
- 4 tablespoons vegetable oil
- 3 cups broccoli stems and florets, stems peeled and cut into 2-inch pieces
- ¼ cup water
- 2 red bell peppers, cored, seeded, and cut into 1-inch-wide strips
- 2 cloves garlic, mashed slightly with the flat side of a knife
- ⅓ cup low-sodium soy sauce
- 1 tablespoon sesame oil
- 2 tablespoons dry sherry
- 2 teaspoons prepared Chinese mustard
- 2 teaspoons cornstarch

Place the onions in a medium-sized saucepan and add the vinegar and enough water to cover the onions. Place the pan over high heat, bring the liquid to a simmer, lower the heat, and cook for 6 to 8 minutes or until the onions are tender. Drain, cool slightly, and slip off the skins.

Heat 2 tablespoons of the oil in a wok or large skillet over high heat. Add the broccoli and toss until well coated with oil. Add the water, cover, and steam the broccoli for 3 minutes. Add the onions and red peppers and cook, uncovered, for an additional 2 to 3 minutes or just until the peppers begin to wilt. Remove the vegetables to a serving dish.

Add the other 2 tablespoons of oil to the wok or skillet and return to moderate heat. Add the garlic and cook until golden, about 3 minutes. Remove the garlic with a slotted spoon. Add the soy sauce, sesame oil, sherry, and mustard; mix to combine. Sprinkle on the cornstarch and stir over moderate heat until the sauce thickens. Pour the sauce over the vegetables and serve.

Broccoli Cheese Casserole

Serves 6

Your Grandma used to make this. Serve it on a cold winter's night, along with a bowl of cream of tomato soup.

- ½ pound sharp Cheddar cheese, cut into 1-inch cubes
- ½ cup milk
- 2 tablespoons Wondra or instant flour

Dash of hot sauce to taste

- 1½ cups finely crushed saltine crackers
- 1 large bunch broccoli (about 1 pound), stems peeled and separated into 1-inch-thick lengths about 4 inches long
- 1 medium onion, coarsely chopped
- ⅓ cup (5⅓ tablespoons) melted butter or margarine

Preheat the oven to 375°F with the rack in the center position. Grease or spray with nonstick vegetable cooking oil a 2-quart casserole dish.

Place the cheese and milk in a small saucepan over medium heat. Bring to a simmer, stirring constantly with a wire whisk. When the cheese melts, add the flour and cook for an additional 3 minutes. Set aside.

Spread half of the cracker crumbs in the bottom of the prepared casserole dish. Arrange the broccoli and onions over the crumbs. Pour the cheese sauce over the vegetables and top with the remaining crumbs. Pour the butter over the crumbs. Bake for 30 to 40 minutes or until the top is browned and the sauce bubbles.

Broccoli Ratatouille

Serves 6 to 8

In this version of the classic French dish, it's important not to overcook the vegetables.

- 1 tablespoon olive oil
- 1 cup thinly sliced Spanish onions or other sweet onions
- 2 cloves garlic, minced
- 1 medium zucchini, cut into 1/4-inch slices
- 1 green bell pepper, cored, seeded, and sliced into thin strips
- 1 1/2 cups broccoli florets, cut into bite-sized pieces
- 1 1/2 cups broccoli stems, peeled and thinly sliced
- One 28-ounce can whole tomatoes, undrained
- 1/4 cup chopped fresh basil, or 1 teaspoon dried basil
- 1/3 cup chopped fresh parsley
- Salt and freshly ground black pepper to taste
- Cooked rice or noodles

In a large skillet or in a microwave in a covered dish, heat the oil and sauté the onions and garlic until translucent. Add the zucchini and sauté for 5 more minutes.

Add the peppers, broccoli, tomatoes, and basil and simmer, covered, until the broccoli is tender, about 5 minutes.

Add the parsley and season with salt and pepper to taste. Serve over rice or noodles.

Broccoli with Mango Chutney and Cashews

Serves 6

With its hint of curry, this dish makes a wonderful accompaniment to broiled or baked fish. Mango chutney is available in the condiment section of your supermarket. Be sure to use unsalted cashews.

- ¼ cup mango chutney
- 3 tablespoons fresh orange juice
- 1 teaspoon cornstarch
- ½ teaspoon curry powder
- 4 cups broccoli stems and florets, stems peeled and sliced diagonally into bite-sized pieces
- ¼ cup toasted unsalted cashew halves

In a 1-quart saucepan over medium heat, mix together the chutney and orange juice. Sprinkle with the cornstarch and curry powder and stir until well mixed. Heat until the mixture comes to a gentle boil.

Add the broccoli, lower the heat, and cover. Simmer for 3 more minutes.

Remove the broccoli to a serving dish and top with cashews.

Coconut Broccoli Stems

Serves 4

This is a spicy vegetarian dish that can be served over rice, cooked lentils, or beans. The addition of cubes of tofu makes it a perfect entrée.

- 2 cups broccoli stems, peeled and chopped into ½-inch pieces
- ¼ cup water plus 1 to 2 tablespoons
- ¾ cup grated fresh coconut, or ½ cup dried unsweetened coconut
- ½ teaspoon ground cumin
- 1 dried red chile
- Salt to taste
- Dash of hot sauce (optional)
- ½ teaspoon cornstarch or rice flour
- ¼ cup yogurt
- Cooked rice

Place the broccoli and the ¼ cup water in a medium-sized saucepan over moderate heat. Cook for 2 minutes or just until the stems are soft. Set aside in the pan.

Place the coconut, cumin, chile, and the 1 tablespoon water in the work bowl of a food processor or blender and process to a thin paste. Add more water if needed. Add salt to taste and hot sauce if desired.

Pour the mixture over the broccoli stems and return the pan to the heat. Sprinkle with the cornstarch, stir to combine, and cook over moderate heat, stirring occasionally, for about 5 minutes. Remove from the heat, stir in the yogurt, and serve hot over rice.

Broccoli Falafel

Serves 6 to 8

This is a baked version of a dish that is usually fried. Delicious served hot or at room temperature, falafel can also be made ahead (up to twenty-four hours), refrigerated, and then reheated in the oven or toaster oven. A recipe for a delicious dipping sauce follows.

- 1/4 cup fine bulgur or cracked wheat
- 1/4 cup boiling water
- 1 tablespoon fresh lemon juice
- 2 cloves garlic, peeled
- 2 cups broccoli stems and florets, stems peeled and cut into 1-inch pieces
- 1/2 teaspoon salt
- 1/2 teaspoon freshly ground black pepper
- One 10-ounce can chick-peas, rinsed and drained
- 1/4 cup grated Parmesan cheese
- 1/2 cup seasoned bread crumbs or stuffing mix
- 1 1/2 cups plain yogurt (regular or low-fat)
- 1/2 cup ground cumin
- 1 tablespoon soy sauce
- Freshly ground black pepper to taste

Soak the bulgur in the water for 45 minutes or until the bulgur is soft. Drain any excess liquid.

Preheat the oven to 450°F with the rack in the center position. Line a baking sheet with aluminum foil.

Place the bulgur and all the remaining ingredients in the work bowl of a food processor or blender and process until well blended. Use a tablespoon to scoop out walnut-sized pieces and use your fingers to shape them into balls. Place them on the prepared sheet and bake for 25 to 30 minutes until golden and crispy.

For the sauce, mix together the yogurt, cumin, soy sauce, and black pepper in a bowl and serve with the falafel.

Indian Dal and Broccoli

Serves 6 to 8

The special Indian ingredients here can be found in ethnic food shops, some health food stores, and occasionally in the gourmet department of large supermarkets. These beans and peas have been split and husked, which means they cook in a short time. In this recipe, the dal takes on a nutty flavor when sautéed, giving the dish a wonderfully mellow taste.

- 3 tablespoons vegetable oil
- 2 teaspoons black mustard seeds
- 1 tablespoon urad dal (black gram beans)
- 1 tablespoon channa dal (yellow gram peas) or yellow split peas
- 4 cups broccoli florets, cut into bite-sized pieces
- ½ teaspoon salt
- 2 to 3 tablespoons water

Heat the oil in a skillet over moderate heat. Add the mustard seeds and dal and sauté for 2 to 3 minutes, shaking the pan briskly back and forth to agitate the dal.

Add the broccoli and stir to mix it into the other ingredients. Sprinkle with salt, add the water as needed, cover the pan, and cook for 5 to 7 minutes. Serve as a vegetable side dish or as a main course along with soup and a salad.

Miso Broccoli

Serves 8

Light miso is an ingredient available in health food stores and the Oriental section of some supermarkets. You can use mild or hot sesame oil, according to how spicy you like it. Daikon is the long white Japanese radish.

    1 teaspoon sesame oil (mild or hot)
    1 tablespoon vegetable oil
    4 cups broccoli stems and florets, stems peeled and thinly sliced on the diagonal, florets cut into large pieces
    2 teaspoons light miso
    1 teaspoon sugar
    ⅓ cup grated daikon (grate on the coarse side of the grater)

Heat the oils in a large skillet and sauté the broccoli over medium-high heat until tender yet still crisp.

Push the broccoli to one side of the skillet. Add the miso and sugar to the center of the pan, stirring until well mixed and the mixture begins to darken. Push the broccoli back to the center and toss until coated with miso. Remove to a serving bowl, garnish with daikon, and serve.

Broccoli with Sesame, Japanese Style

Serves 8

This quickly sautéed dish is flavored with dashi, which is made from dried bonito tuna and kelp. It is readily available in health food stores and many Oriental markets. The broccoli stems are peeled, cut into matchsticks, and served uncooked with the sauce.

- 1/4 cup sesame seeds
- 1 tablespoon dashi (or substitute fish stock)
- 2 teaspoons tamari soy sauce
- 4 cups broccoli stems and florets, stems peeled and cut into matchsticks, florets cut into bite-sized pieces

Spread the sesame seeds in a small frying pan. Cook over medium heat until light brown and you can smell the sesame aroma. Shake the pan occasionally.

Mix the dashi according to directions and measure out 1 tablespoon into a bowl. Add the soy sauce and sesame seeds. Mix well and pour over the broccoli.

Broccoli: It's Good for You

There is potential good news for all broccoli lovers—news beyond how good it tastes. Researchers at The Johns Hopkins University have been studying a naturally existing chemical found in broccoli called sulforaphane that kindles the activity of critical enzymes in the cells known to help combat tumors. These findings were published in two papers in an issue of *The Proceedings of the National Academy of Sciences.* While the final word isn't in yet, there are other important reasons to eat broccoli.

Our favorite vegetable is beautiful to behold, irresistibly delicious, wondrously versatile, adorably adaptable, and a 2.6-ounce serving (approximately 1 cup) delivers 130 percent of the U.S. Recommended Daily Amount of vitamin C, 20 percent of the USRDA vitamin A, and a healthy dose of fiber as well. Broccoli also contains vitamin E and vitamin K, a little iron, and is a good source of calcium—ounce for ounce almost as much as milk.

Not only is our favorite vegetable always in season, but it is also very low in calories—only 40 calories per cup—so if you watch what you put on it, your scale will continue to sing out good news. When eaten raw, it's an especially great source of fiber. Don't laugh! Try peeling off the outer skin of several medium-sized stalks, cut the inner part into slices, and enjoy. Add it to your crudité plate.

BROCCOLI
Main Courses

Broccoli Turkey Divan

Serves 6

This is the epitome of comfort food—homey and delicious. You can use leftover slices of turkey or buy it from the deli.

- 1 pound broccoli, stems peeled and cut into thin spears 4 inches long
- 6 slices turkey (4 inches by 1/4 inch)
- 3 tablespoons butter or margarine
- 1/4 cup all-purpose flour
- 2 cups chicken broth, or 1 chicken or vegetable bouillion cube dissolved in 2 cups hot water
- 2 cups grated medium-sharp Cheddar cheese
- 1 tablespoon Worcestershire sauce
- 1/4 cup chopped fresh parsley

Preheat the oven to 350°F. Spray a 2-quart casserole with nonstick vegetable cooking oil. Line the bottom with the broccoli and cover the broccoli with the turkey slices.

Melt the butter over medium heat in a small, heavy-bottomed saucepan. Sprinkle with the flour, whisking continuously until the flour is absorbed. Slowly add the broth and continue whisking until the sauce is smooth and thickened.

Remove the sauce from the heat, sprinkle with the cheese, and whisk until the cheese melts. Pour the sauce over the turkey and bake, uncovered, for 30 minutes.

Crisp Broccoli-Potato Pancake

Serves 6

A nonstick pan is an essential tool when making this pan-sized pancake. You can grate the broccoli and potatoes by hand with a metal grater, or with the grating blade of a food processor.

- 1 tablespoon olive oil
- 3 broccoli stems, peeled and grated lengthwise (1½ cups)
- 2 medium peeled potatoes, grated lengthwise (2 cups)
- ½ cup chopped onions
- 1 tablespoon capers, drained

Heat the oil in a 10-inch nonstick skillet over medium heat.

In a bowl, toss together the broccoli stems, potatoes, onions, and capers. Add them to the hot pan and press down firmly with the back of a spatula.

Cook for 10 minutes without stirring or turning. Loosen the edges occasionally, and shake the pan to loosen the vegetables. Gently lift the edges, and when the underside is deep golden brown and crispy, remove the pan from the heat. Loosen the edges, shake to loosen, then cover with a large flat plate. Flip the pan and plate together. Lift off the pan. Slide the pancake back into the pan and continue cooking for about 10 more minutes or until the second side is golden and crispy.

Slide the pancake onto a serving plate. Cut into wedges and serve.

Broccoli–Smoked Turkey Rolls

Serves 6

This is a terrific buffet dish that makes a stunning presentation. The recipe can be doubled or tripled and it can be assembled ahead (up to eight hours), refrigerated, and then baked just before serving.

- 8 slices smoked turkey, cut ¼ inch thick
- 1 large egg, beaten
- 2 cups broccoli stems, peeled, chopped, and steamed or microwaved for 2 minutes or until just tender
- ¾ cup regular or skim-milk ricotta cheese
- 2 tablespoons grated Romano cheese plus 3 tablespoons for the topping
- ½ cup grated mozzarella cheese
- One 16-ounce can tomato sauce

Preheat the oven to 350°F with the rack in the center position. Grease or spray with nonstick vegetable cooking oil an 11-inch × 7-inch baking pan.

In a bowl, combine the egg, broccoli, and cheeses.

Divide the filling among the turkey slices and spread over half of each slice. Fold the other half over the filling and then roll up each piece, placing the roll in the prepared pan as you complete it.

Pour the tomato sauce over the rolls and top with the 3 tablespoons grated cheese. Bake for 30 to 40 minutes or until the top is brown and the sauce bubbling.

Broccoli and Chicken with Cashews

Serves 6

You've had this in Chinese restaurants. Wait until you taste how much more delicious it is when you make it at home.

- 1 tablespoon soy sauce
- 1 tablespoon dry sherry
- 1 teaspoon sugar
- 4 boneless, skinless chicken breasts, sliced into 1-inch strips
- 2 tablespoons peanut oil
- 1 teaspoon minced fresh ginger
- 2 cloves garlic, minced
- 4 cups broccoli stems and florets, stems peeled and thinly sliced on the diagonal, florets cut into bite-sized pieces
- 2 teaspoons water
- 1 tablespoon hoisin sauce
- 1/2 cup whole roasted cashew nuts
- 3 cups cooked rice
- 2 scallions, green and white parts, chopped

In a bowl, mix together the soy sauce, sherry, and sugar. Add the chicken and set aside.

Heat the oil in a wok or skillet over high heat. Add the ginger and garlic and toss until just golden but not brown. Add the chicken strips and marinade and sauté until browned, about 3 minutes. Remove the chicken strips to a serving dish.

Add the broccoli and water to the wok. Cover and steam for 2 minutes.

Return the chicken to the wok. Add the hoisin sauce and cashews. Toss quickly to mix, then remove from heat because hoisin sauce will burn easily. Serve over rice, garnished with scallions.

Chicken Broccoli Medallions

Serves 6

A fancy-looking dish with only three ingredients, this is great hot or cold. It also makes a wonderful picnic or tailgate meal.

    3 whole chicken breasts, skins removed, halved, and
      pounded to ½-inch thickness
    ½ cup Broccoli Pesto (page 23)
    ½ cup dry white wine
    1 tablespoon butter or margarine

Preheat the oven to 400°F. Spray a shallow 13-inch × 11-inch baking dish with nonstick vegetable cooking oil.

Spread 2 tablespoons pesto over each chicken breast and roll up tightly, securing with a toothpick before placing it seam side down in the prepared dish.

Dot with butter, add the wine, and cover loosely with aluminum foil. Bake for 40 minutes, removing the foil for the last 10 minutes of cooking.

Cool slightly, remove the toothpicks, then use a long sharp knife to cut each roll into four to five slices before serving.

Broccoli-Chicken-Cheese Roll-ups

Serves 8

You can substitute skim-milk ricotta in this recipe if you wish. Served with a green salad and freshly baked bread, this makes an easy family supper.

- 8 boneless, skinless chicken breasts
- ½ cup bottled Italian dressing
- 1 cup chopped broccoli stems and florets, stems peeled and steamed or microwaved for 2 minutes or until just tender
- 1 cup regular or skim-milk ricotta cheese
- ¼ cup chopped fresh parsley
- ¼ cup sliced scallions, green and white parts
- 1 large egg or ¼ cup egg substitute
- ½ cup dry white wine or chicken broth
- Salt and freshly ground black pepper to taste

Place the chicken breasts in a shallow dish, pour over the salad dressing, cover with plastic wrap, and refrigerate for at least 30 minutes or as long as 3 hours.

Preheat the oven to 350°F with the rack in the center position. Spray a 9-inch × 13-inch baking dish with nonstick vegetable cooking oil.

In a bowl, mix together the broccoli, ricotta, parsley, scallions, egg, salt, and pepper.

Divide the filling among the chicken breasts and spread it out almost to the edges. Roll the chicken around the filling, secure with a toothpick, and place seam side down in the prepared baking pan.

Add the wine, cover loosely with aluminum foil, and bake for 45 minutes, removing the foil during the last 10 minutes of cooking. Remove the toothpicks before serving.

Pasta with Broccoli, Pesto, and Chicken

Serves 4

Here's an easy one-pot meal where the chicken and pasta are cooked together. Select thick pasta such as fettuccine or macaroni.

    1 pound fettuccine

    2 whole boneless, skinless chicken breasts, cut into
      1½-inch pieces

    2 tablespoons olive or vegetable oil

    ⅓ cup Broccoli Pesto (page 23)

    ¼ cup roasted red peppers or pimientos

    1 cup bite-sized broccoli florets, steamed or
      microwaved for 2 minutes or until just tender

Cook the pasta together with the chicken pieces in a large pot of boiling water until the chicken is cooked through and the pasta is tender, about 12 minutes. Drain.

In a serving bowl, toss the chicken and pasta with the oil. Add the pesto, peppers, and broccoli. Toss again and serve.

Broccoli and Vermicelli

Serves 4 to 6

In this recipe, you can substitute plum tomatoes for the cherry tomatoes, or if local tomatoes are in season, use them.

- 1 pound vermicelli
- 4 cups broccoli florets, cut into bite-sized pieces and steamed or microwaved for 2 minutes or until just tender
- 2 tablespoons olive oil
- 2 cloves garlic, minced
- 1 cup cherry tomatoes, halved

Cook the vermicelli according to package directions. Drain.

While the vermicelli is cooking, heat the oil in a skillet over medium-high heat and sauté the garlic until light golden. Add the vermicelli and broccoli and toss.

Remove to a serving dish, add the tomatoes, and toss before serving.

Broccoli Pizza

Serves 4 as an appetizer or
2 to 3 as a main course

You can use store-bought pizza dough or make your own. Try adding strips of lean ham or smoked turkey to this nouvelle-style pizza.

Dough for one 8- to 10-inch pizza crust

2 tablespoons olive oil

¼ cup Broccoli Pesto (page 23)

¼ cup red bell peppers, cored, seeded, and cut into thin strips

1 cup broccoli florets, cut into 1-inch pieces and steamed or microwaved for 2 minutes or until just tender

¼ cup feta cheese, crumbled

1 cup grated cheese (such as mozzarella or fontina)

Preheat the oven to 425°F. Sprinkle a pizza pan or baking sheet with 2 tablespoons cornmeal.

Stretch the pizza dough into a 8- to 10-inch circle. Spread the dough with half the oil and then the pesto. Distribute the peppers and broccoli evenly over the pesto. Crumble the feta over the vegetables. Mix together the other cheeses and sprinkle them over the pizza.

Drizzle with the remaining oil and bake for 12 to 15 minutes. Slice into wedges and serve.

Broccoli Frittata

Serves 2

A frittata is a large unfolded omelet that gets cut into wedges to serve several people for a light supper or substantial brunch dish. It's also great as an appetizer when cut into small squares. Remember to use a nonstick skillet when you make this.

    3 large eggs
   ¾ cup milk
    1 tablespoon olive oil
    1 cup thinly sliced Spanish onions
    1 clove garlic, minced
    1 tablespoon chopped fresh oregano, or ½ teaspoon dried oregano
    4 large leaves fresh basil, chopped, or ½ teaspoon dried basil
    1 red bell pepper, cored, seeded, and sliced into long thin strips
    2 cups chopped broccoli stems and florets, stems peeled, steamed or microwaved for 2 minutes or until just tender, and well drained
    1 small potato, peeled and thinly sliced into ½-inch pieces
   Salt and freshly ground black pepper to taste

In a bowl, beat together the eggs and milk. Set aside.

In a 10-inch nonstick skillet, heat and swirl the oil to completely cover the bottom. Add the onions, garlic, and herbs and sauté over medium-high heat until the onions just start to turn clear.

Reduce the heat to medium. Add the pepper strips and broccoli, and toss until well mixed. Give the eggs and milk another stir and pour them over the vegetables.

Cook the mixture without stirring. As the eggs start to set, loosen the edges with a spatula and lift them to check the browning on the bottom. Reduce the heat if the bottom starts to get too brown. When the top is set, loosen the edges and gently shake the pan to loosen the frittata. Cover the pan with a large flat plate and flip the pan over the plate so the frittata is on the plate. Slide the frittata back into the pan and brown the other side for 10 minutes.

Loosen the edges, shake the pan to loosen the frittata, and slide the frittata onto a serving plate. Season with salt and pepper, cut into wedges, and serve.

Broccoli Enchiladas

Serves 10

This is a low-cost, quick-to-prepare dish that can be doubled or tripled to feed a crowd. Serve it with black bean soup for a hearty meal. A variation with beans follows.

Two 10-ounce cans enchilada sauce

1 bunch broccoli, separated into 20 thin stalks, stems peeled and trimmed to 4 inches, steamed or microwaved for 2 minutes or until just tender

10 enchilada-sized corn or flour tortillas

2½ cups grated Colby or Monterey Jack cheese

Preheat the oven to 350°F. Spray a 9-inch by 13-inch baking dish with nonstick vegetable cooking oil. Pour half a can of enchilada sauce over the bottom of the baking dish.

Place 2 stalks of broccoli, stems overlapping, in the center of each tortilla. Sprinkle each with 2 heaping tablespoons of grated cheese. Roll up the tortillas and place them seam side down in the baking dish.

Cover with the remaining enchilada sauce. Top with the remaining cheese and bake for 45 minutes.

Broccoli Enchiladas with Beans

Heat 2 teaspoons olive oil in a nonstick pan over medium-high heat. Add 1 minced clove garlic, and 1 cup coarsely chopped onions and sauté until tender. Add two 13-ounce cans red kidney drained beans and cook, stirring occasionally, until all of the liquid is evaporated and the beans are well softened.

Place about ⅓ cup cooked beans in the center of each enchilada. Top with 2 stalks of broccoli and 2 heaping tablespoons of grated cheese. Roll up and place seam side down in the baking dish. Pour over the remaining sauce and top with the remaining cheese. Bake for 45 minutes.

Garnish with sour cream, if desired, and serve.

Broccoli Fajitas

Serves 6

A fajita is a mixture of sautéed vegetables and meat served rolled up in warm tortillas and topped with guacamole and sour cream, if you wish. Tortillas are available in the refrigerated cases of your supermarket. You may substitute strips of chicken for the beef in this recipe.

  2 tablespoons olive oil

  2 cloves garlic, minced

  1 medium Spanish onion, chopped

  1 red bell pepper, cored, seeded, and cut into thin strips

1½ pounds beef, cut into thin strips (sirloin, if available)

  2 canned chile peppers, minced (mild or hot, depending on your taste)

  4 cups broccoli stems and florets, stems peeled, sliced into thin spears, and steamed or microwaved for 2 minutes or until just tender

  2 to 3 tablespoons chili powder

 ¼ teaspoon cayenne pepper

  1 large tomato, chopped

 ½ cup guacamole

 ½ cup sour cream

 12 warm corn or flour tortillas

Heat the oil in a large skillet over medium heat. Sauté the garlic and onions until tender. Add the red pepper, beef, and spices. Stir-fry until the beef is cooked through.

Add the broccoli and stir-fry until it is well coated.

Serve on warm tortillas, topped with tomatoes, guacamole, and sour cream, if desired. Roll up to eat.

Indian Broccoli Stems

Serves 2

This mildly spicy dish makes a great vegetarian main course.

- ⅓ cup moong dal (mung beans) (available in health food and Indian markets and specialty stores)
- 1 cup water
- 2 cups broccoli stems, peeled and chopped into 1-inch pieces
- ½ teaspoon garam masala (available in health food and Indian markets and specialty stores)
- 2 tablespoons water
- 3 cups cooked rice, red beans, or chick-peas

Add the mung beans to the water in a heavy-bottomed saucepan and bring to a boil. Cover and reduce the heat to medium. Cook for 10 minutes, stirring occasionally, until the dal is tender but not mushy.

Add the broccoli stems and garam masala. Add water if the dal seems very dry. Cook over low heat, stirring occasionally, until the broccoli is tender, about 10 minutes. Serve over rice, red beans, or chick-peas.

Crustless Broccoli Quiche

Makes 1 10-inch quiche, serves 6 to 8

The hardest part of this dish—the crust—is eliminated here, making for a speedy, no-fail luncheon dish. Serve it with a salad and soup and you have an informal yet delicious supper—one that can be made in minutes. This can be made up to three hours ahead and served at room temperature.

      1 tablespoon olive oil
      1 cup thinly sliced onions
    One 10-ounce package mushrooms, thinly sliced
      2 cups broccoli stems, peeled and chopped into
        1/2-inch pieces
      8 ounces Swiss cheese, grated
      4 large eggs
      1 cup milk
    1/4 teaspoon ground nutmeg
    1/4 teaspoon freshly ground black pepper

Preheat the oven to 425°F. Spray a 10-inch glass pie plate with nonstick vegetable cooking oil.

Heat the oil in a 10″ skillet. Add the onions and mushrooms and sauté over medium-high heat for about 10 to 15 minutes or until caramelized and golden brown but not burned, and the liquid has evaporated. Spread the mixture over the bottom of the pie plate and press down with a metal spatula. Distribute chopped broccoli over the mushroom mixture and sprinkle on the grated cheese.

Beat together the eggs, milk, and spices. Pour this mixture over the cheese.

Bake for 15 minutes, then reduce the heat to 350°F and continue baking for another 10 to 15 minutes or until the top turns a deep golden color and a knife inserted in the center comes out clean. Serve hot or at room temperature.

Potato-Broccoli- Cheese Bake

Serves 6

A perfect down-home dish that will warm your family and friends come winter.

> 4 cups peeled potato slices, 1½ inches thick
> 3 cups broccoli stems and florets, stems peeled and coarsely chopped
> 4 tablespoons butter or margarine
> 3 tablespoons all-purpose flour
> 1½ cups milk
> 2 cups grated Cheddar cheese
> 4 to 5 dashes hot sauce
> ⅔ cup finely crushed whole-grained crackers
> ¼ cup sliced almonds

Preheat the oven to 375°F. Spray a 2-quart casserole with nonstick vegetable cooking oil.

Arrange half the potato slices on the bottom of the casserole. Cover with half of the broccoli. Arrange the second half of the potatoes over the broccoli. Cover with the second half of the broccoli.

Melt the butter in a heavy-bottomed saucepan over medium heat. Sprinkle on the flour, whisking continuously. Continue whisking and slowly add the milk. Whisk until the mixture is thickened and smooth.

Remove the pan from the heat and sprinkle in the cheese,

whisking until melted. Add hot sauce to taste. Pour the cheese sauce over the broccoli and potatoes.

Mix the crackers and almonds and sprinkle over the top of the casserole.

Bake for 1 hour or until the potatoes are tender and the top is crusty.

Baked Cod and Broccoli
Serves 4

If you are looking for dinner in a hurry, try this three-ingredient dish. You can substitute any white fillets (such as flounder or sole) for the cod. You can even make this over a campfire if you cook it in a disposable pan.

> 1½ **pounds cod or other whitefish fillets**
> 2 **to 3 ounces medium-sharp Cheddar cheese, sliced ¼ inch thick**
> 2 **cups broccoli stems and florets, stems peeled and coarsely chopped**

Rinse the fish, pat it dry, and place it flat in an 8-cup ovenproof dish sprayed with nonstick vegetable cooking oil. Lay cheese slices down the center of the fish, covering almost to the edges. Place the broccoli on the cheese.

Cover the dish with aluminum foil and bake at 325°F for 20 to 30 minutes, depending on the thickness of the fish. The fish will flake easily when done.

Broccoli and Fish Grilled in Foil

Serves 4

Here is an unusually beautiful fish preparation. The long thin shreds of vegetables give it an Oriental appearance and the seasonings add a delectable zing. It's a perfect summertime dish for when outdoor cooking is more appealing than turning on the oven.

Two 1-pound cod or other mild whitefish fillets

2 tablespoons olive oil

2 tablespoons fresh rosemary, or 2 teaspoons dried rosemary

6 slivers (1 inch by 4 inches) peeled fresh ginger

2 cups broccoli stems and florets, stems peeled

1 small yellow summer squash, grated lengthwise

1 small zucchini, grated lengthwise

1/2 green bell pepper, cored, seeded, and coarsely chopped

1/4 cup soy sauce

1 scallion, green and white parts, sliced

6 very thin lemon slices

Spray two 3-foot long pieces of heavy-duty aluminum foil with nonstick vegetable cooking oil or brush with vegetable oil. Rinse the fish, pat it dry, and place each fillet in the center of an 18-inch piece of heavy-duty aluminum foil.

Spread each fish fillet with 1 tablespoon oil. Sprinkle each with half the rosemary. Top each with slivers of ginger. Cover each with grated summer squash, then zucchini. Sprinkle with green peppers and scallions. Pour on the soy sauce and add lemon slices.

Seal the foil tightly into a package and place on the grill. Cook for 20 to 30 minutes, depending on the hotness of your coals, until the vegetables are tender and the fish flakes easily. Be careful to open the foil slowly because escaping steam is hot.

NOTE: You may substitute 1 medium-sized carrot, grated lengthwise, for the squash and 4 tablespoons fresh dill for the rosemary.

Broccoli Crepes with Orange Liqueur

Serves 6 to 8

A real showstopper! The orange liqueur is a wonderful complement to the flavors of whole wheat in the crepes. You can make the
crepes ahead of time (up to twenty-four hours) and refrigerate
them until you are ready to prepare the dish. The filling is best if
prepared just before serving.

- 1 whole large egg plus 2 egg whites
- 1 cup buttermilk
- ½ cup water
- 3 tablespoons vegetable oil
- ⅓ cup whole wheat flour
- ⅔ cup all-purpose white flour
- ½ teaspoon baking soda
- ¼ teaspoon baking powder
- 1 teaspoon sugar
- ½ teaspoon salt

- 2 tablespoons vegetable oil
- 1½ teaspoons cornstarch
- Finely grated rind of 1 orange
- ⅔ cup fresh orange juice
- 1 tablespoon orange liqueur
- 1 pound broccoli separated into thin spears, stems peeled and trimmed to 4 inches
- ½ cup sour cream (optional)
- ½ cup sliced almonds

Combine the first ten ingredients in a blender or food processor and process for 1 to 2 minutes until thoroughly mixed. Let the batter stand, refrigerated, for 30 minutes.

Spray a nonstick crepe pan with nonstick vegetable cooking oil and place over medium-high heat. Pour 4-inch crepes and cook until the underside is golden and the top is no longer wet. Loosen the edges, if necessary, shake the pan, and slide the crepe out. Flip the crepe over, return to the pan, and cook for 10 more seconds.

For the filling, heat the oil over medium heat in a heavy-bottomed pan. Add the cornstarch, orange rind, orange juice, and orange liqueur. Whisk until thickened.

Add the broccoli spears and mix until well coated with the sauce. Cover the pan and simmer on low heat for 2 to 3 minutes or until the broccoli is tender yet still crisp.

Place 2 to 3 broccoli spears in the center of each crepe. Top with 1 tablespoon sour cream. Fold up the crepe. Drizzle a little sauce from the pan over the folded crepe and sprinkle with almonds. Serve immediately.

Broccoli with Scallops

Serves 4

You can use either bay or sea scallops in this recipe. If you select the large sea scallops, cut them in halves or quarters before cooking. This tastes great served over rice, pasta, or couscous.

    1 tablespoon vegetable oil
    1 clove garlic, mashed with the flat side of a knife
1 1/2 pounds scallops, rinsed and patted dry
    2 teaspoons cornstarch
  1/4 to 1/2 teaspoon freshly ground black pepper
    3 cups broccoli florets with 3-inch stems, stems
      peeled, steamed for 2 to 3 minutes, drained, and
      kept warm in a covered pan or low oven.

Heat the oil in a wok or skillet over high heat and sauté the garlic until golden. Remove the garlic and discard.

Add the scallops and stir-fry until they are white and firm, about 3 to 5 minutes.

Remove the scallops with a slotted spoon and pile them in the center of a round serving platter.

Sprinkle the cooking liquid in the skillet with the cornstarch and raise the heat to high, stirring constantly until the sauce thickens. Stir in the pepper.

Place the steamed broccoli around the scallops. Drizzle the sauce over all and serve at once.

Index